DESIGNED BY CREATIVE SKETCHBOOKS STUDIO FOR CREATIVE JOURNALS FACTORY.

THANK YOU WE HOPE YOU LIKED YOUR SKETCHBOOK PLEASE WRITE YOUR REVIEW, IT MEANS A LOT TO US!

FIND OTHER BEAUTIFUL JOURNALS, DIARIES AND NOTEBOOKS AT:

www.CreativeJournalsFactory.com

JOURNALS - DIARIES - NOTEBOOKS - COLORING BOOKS

Made in United States
Orlando, FL
03 April 2024